REFINED FOR PURPOSE

Written by: Maria Ushery

Table Of Contents

Acknowledgements iii

Cover Girl 1

Show up 5

Split ends 8

The Prodigal 11

Zero 14

Perfectionism my story my storm 17

About the Author 19

Acknowledgements

This has been a very Challenging Journey for me, there were many dark days, however, it was also rewarding witnessing the cover girl uncovering and removing the layers. And there have been some individuals who have been my motivation, my encouragers, and pushers and my reasons to never give up; they are my three children and Mother Queen Esther Ushery, she's the strongest women I have ever met, she has always pushed me to become greater than her, and during my seasons of starting task and not completing them, she would affectionately say, "Now Ree, you need to complete some things" Well, I made her SUPER proud this year, I love you Mom! My three children, Rashanna, Rashan, Rashid and Grandchildren McKenzie and Mali.

My first love, Rashan (Pooker) he stole my heart the first sight of me, looking him in the face he's spontaneous, brave, adventurous and intelligent, the Prophet. My one and only Daughter Rashanna (Molly) she's the younger me and so many ways, although the 45 years old me absolutely despise to admit it. Lol!

This Lady is my scholar, I am proud of her in every way, she is brave, intelligent, very hard working, loyal, she's the epitome of GO HARD OR GO HOME! About her business and an Absolutely great mother to my Nan! Rashid (ush) He's my soon to be NBA player, I am proud of him, he's a hard worker, gentle giant, very loyal, intelligent. He rather plays basketball than eat lol.

My two Grand girls are both absolutely adorable, I love them with my whole life McKenzie (Kenzie) Mali (Nan). I love my Children and Grandchildren with all that is within me.

Cover Girl

Makeup can be a woman's best friend or her worst nightmare. Let's chat about the why behind the cover girl! Some choose to wear it as a camouflage to appear less noticeable, because of insecurities, some to be seductive, wanting to be noticed and more attractive and to become more confident socially and assertive. During the month of May my life was at a standstill everything I mean everything slowed down right before my eyes, I didn't feel like I was in the month of May not the Month of May that they say bring forth May flowers, neither was I coming out of the of April that bring forth showers, but the Month of May that brought forth draught and defeat. I felt like a car driving on "E" pushing, hoping and praying that the car didn't stop on I95 that is exactly how I felt during that time as I was trying to keep it together.

I voluntarily resigned from my 3rd Job within a 12-month time period, Life personally was getting to be overwhelming, and I didn't even want to work, I have worked for years, but now my emotional tolerance decreased. And I knew that whenever I was ready to return back to the workforce, I would have absolutely no issue with getting an interview and being offered the employment opportunity within 48 hours of the interview. After all

God has graced me when it comes to employment I could get employment opportunities fervently, as well as help others when and if they're in the market, however as mentioned earlier. Things were slow for me, I felt like my life was reverting back to the year 2000 when I didn't have much of anything. As if that wasn't enough during that time. My vehicle was involved in attempted hijacking while my 17-year-old Son was at the Gas pump.

That was a situation within its self, things became even slower after that incident, the length of time between the adjuster coming out to asses the car and check being cut from the third-party carrier and the actual repairs took approximately 61 days, as if that wasn't enough, when I got the car back, I didn't work, the car experience water damage creating permanent issue with the electrical system....

Things increasingly became slower for me. I began to say within myself this is abnormal, well it wasn't my normal and I felt extremely defeated, depleted and frustrated as life slowed down to the point I was on pause within my personal life, there was no movement, no employers found interest in my cover letter and resume I began to question God's love for me(personally), I was doing all the things pertaining to the Ministry and thriving spiritually, but personal life wasn't producing much fruit at all. I had questions, how did I get here?

I was there because I allowed all the outward accomplishment to define who I was and where I was going, God allowed it all to slow down and take a sudden stop. He wanted me to rely on him to be my source and the material things to serve as resources.

So, I was stripped from it all and it was out of my hands and control. 2017 Nissan Maximum sitting in the drive unable to start up. Absolutely no job leads this can't be me! I am still serving the people of God encourage them and pushing them, but I was still slowly waiting. And during that time of the low and slow valley for me The light bulb went off, but it didn't just go off within in me, but the light was shining right on me exposing the silent battles of self-acceptance, opinions of others, self-image, significant weight gain of 45 pounds after having WLS in 2015 and struggling with perfectionism. I was in need of deliverance, OMG! I thought I was healed and delivered, but to my surprise the cover girl was exposed no more cover ups. I asked God what is perfectionism? He led me to look up the definition for clarity and search began. Perfectionism is when a person has a tendency to set excessively high standards for oneself and others. I wanted everything about me to be perfect. *Psalms 18:30 As for God, his way is perfect: The Lord's word is flawless; he shields all who take refuge in him (NIV).* It was clear to me that I was the cover girl, the girl that was hiding behind the material things and the Mac foundation, Royal Secrets lip gloss, lipstick and lip-liner, Love Lash mink eyelashes along with the entire makeup palette.

I didn't leave home without the makeup, not because it looked beautiful while wearing it and it did, but because I didn't like what I saw without it. I had an issue with being seen in public and not all put together, I wanted to be PERFECT when it pertained to my appearance, whew, the cover girl! I wouldn't take photos without having on my makeup, yes me the cover girl.

I was struggling with pride and did not realize it, yup! The Pastor needing deliverance from pride. *1 John 2:16 For everything in the world- the lust of the flesh, the lust the eyes, and the pride of life- comes not from the father but from the world. (NIV)* after he revealed to me what I was dealing with, Reality began to settle in, I am a hot mess! My journey of transitioning began on a Tuesday morning at 6:35am the daily vlogging and early mornings as I did my daily walks. Without makeup, without nice clothes and all the other material things that provided me with false confidence. The Journey of transitioning my identity as the cover girl began, I initially thought that I was on a weightless Journey to shed the few pounds that I picked up during the pandemic, but to my surprise, it wasn't the physical pounds that needed to be shedding, but the emotional weight, the cover girl was being transformed, healed and made whole one step as at a time, I was receiving my healing in front of the world not in private. Sometime what we've hid from we will need to face, no more camouflaging. Journey with me as I discover what all the hype was about with the makeup and what was I really hiding from, The purpose of the Primer is to fill up the pores, bumpy textures, and small creases to make the face more even and easier to work with helping the skin to become a blank canvas, with the primer I could hid who God created me to be and I created my own reality, hiding who you I really was smoothing out all of the rough edges about me, the rough edges that distinctly makes me who God has created me to be temporarily, and not addressing the issue of the unhealthy me, the me that struggled with perfectionism, and the foundation that helps with creating an even complexion along with covering the flaws, the will assist with not seeing that there is some contradictory areas within you that need to be addressed and not covered up, the lashes serviced as an awning to hide me in plain sight, the lip products hid the non-pigmentation of my lips, again all covered up from my reality. The cover girl made the decision, no more cover ups and healed from within.

Psalm 139:13-14 NIV for you created my inmost being you knit me together in my mother's womb. I praise you because I am fearfully and wonderfully made; your works are wonderful. I know that fully well. I know I embrace who God has created me to be as he knitted me together in my mother's womb, I the cover girl was fearfully and wonderfully made. I am enough, the cover girl now, confidently wears the makeup as an enhancer not as a band aid. And through all of that Romans 8:28 For we know that all things work together for them that love the lord and are the called according to his purpose. The drought, the slowness and embarrassing moments, it all worked together for my good. All that I was faced with was a part of my process of healing from the cover girl to become uncovered. I am good now!

Show Up

There are several ways for a person to show up or arrive at a particular place. I simply needed to show up for me, I needed to arise to the occasion that's been waiting for me for so long, my next level was waiting for me. After battling with procrastination stagnation for so many years, I was over it! I'm sure God was heaven saying what is she about to start and not finish this time.

I was a habitual quitter, I should have received a bronze medal for starting projects, school, business etc.…and then stopping. I was great at pushing others into their purposes and whatever they needed me to assist them with to accomplish their desired goals I had them covered, however it's time for me to show up, I challenged myself to show up for me. I began to challenge myself with changing my mind, if you change your mind, you will change your perspective. The discipline and boot camp began, I challenged myself with consistency and compliance short term goals first, for an example.

I created personal challenges for myself and I didn't share with anyone as I didn't want to receive accolades from others or their expectation of me and my desired goals. I challenged myself with making coffee at home for 30 days and not perching any outside coffees, and challenged myself to exercise every morning rain, shine or sun. This is just to name a few. With these short-term goals, I began to build a tolerance for myself. I was showing up for myself. My goals began to aggressively become my reality. my next level is waiting for me, there are many people that will benefit from me just simply showing up. I once heard someone say that the grave yard is filled with gifts, dreams, talent, excuse of I should have or I could have. I refuse to allow that to be my story I am showing up and whenever my time expires, I will die empty after fulfilling all that I was purposed to fulfill by God's grace. As my mind began to change and the way view myself began to elevate too, disciplining myself with those changes allowed me to know that I can do anything I put my mind to small or big, these changes made me more discipled and determined to show up. Acts *26:16(NIV) Now get up and stand on your feet. I have appeared to you to appoint you as a servant and as a witness of what you have seen and will see.*

In this passage of scripture Jesus is speaking Paul after he was transformed from Saul to Paul while on the road to Damascus. Jesus is commissioning him to get up show up and do what he's been called to do. You next level is waiting on you, there are people that God has divinely assigned for us to connect with and cross paths with during our life's journey, they are our destiny helpers. Show up for you, show up for Christ!

If you've ever experience rejection after rejection denial after denial and you felt as it nothing was working out for you. That will push you to changing the narrative of your life, I can remember receiving rejections for positions that I had the experience for but not the education, it was painful to go through, however I had to make the decision to change my story.

I returned back to school, because I never wanted to be denied for not having a piece of paper when I had over 20 years of experience, I had to show up for me not for them, understand that lifer will require you to show up differently, your arrival will not always be the same. Imagine working on a job for 30 years, and the employer informs you that the decision has been made to lay you off or simply terminate your position immediately. Or if you're leasing a rental property and the owner of the property says to you unfortunately, we're selling the property.

Both of those situations are very unfortunate, not for the employer or the owner of the property, but for the individual that was faced with the devastation of the loss, in that case you will need to show up for you, place your self in a position that something of that magnitude will never happen again, its now time to prepare for home ownership and entrepreneurship. Those are just a few examples the list of rejections is longer; however, the purpose is not to focus on the losses, but to place emphasis on the what is ahead. Arise to the occasion, your next level is waiting for you.

Split Ends

Let's talk about it, I have heard the word split ends throughout my entire life and witnessed them in my own hair and others, that the word indeed is a legitimate word, WOW! Trichophilia's, actinotrichia is the actual medical term for split ends.... We know it's the ends of the hair that split due to stress, excessive heat or chemical damage. Interesting enough... I can relate to this from two perspectives, let's talk split ends.

The first time I discovered that I had split ends in my hair due to poor hair maintenance was at the age of sixteen, due to my ignorance of the importance of cutting the split ends I continued to impose more damage to the hair and or just cover it up with hair extensions, and when I would remove the hair extensions and see the split ends again I would ignore the issue and the additional damages that I was inflicting on the hair, who care when you can just add hair, years began to pass and I was not a good steward over my hair, we all know that hair is a Women's crown and she's suppose to take great care of the crown, but when your living reckless you lack the sensitivity to the important things in life. Throughout my life I would wear my hair out without the extensions. I also had a time when I cut all of the hair off and was wearing my hair very closely cut and I loved it. I then discovered that the hair was thinning in a few areas of the hair, but I continued on that journey for a while and loved every moment of it.

I can recall being in Church around the early 2000's and on of the Brothers began to speak on women's hair and what the Lord revealed to him regarding the hair glues and the importance of not adding the extensions well, of course I said to myself "he needs to mind his business and worry about his wife's hair" I remember this like it was yesterday, we all were just sitting in the sanctuary having conversation and he says " God said you all need to stop using the hair glue in your hair because it's going to begin to damage and cause balding" I rolled my eyes so hard, ugh here goes "Mr., know it all". Well! Years later I experienced the very thing that I rolled my eyes at, Ha Ha Ha.

    I was affected by the glue. So here we are at least 19 years later and I desire to now wear my crown free! I made the decision to address what I have been running from since 16 years old, taking care of the crown. I made the bold decision to go to the salon and finally deal with the split ends and cut all the dead hair off and start fresh, and boy ole boy does it feel good. I am free!

    There were several times throughout my life that the split ends weren't just in the form of my hair but I was also experiencing Trichophilia's and schizotrichia in my life not addressing the damaged areas within my life and just going about life as if there were

    no split ends, but how many of us know, if you do not handle the issues the issues will handle you, everything cannot be handled just by prayer and emotionalist. There are times in your life were you need to do some work, just like you have to cut the split ends from your hair or the hair will continue to be damaged and never grow, you will also need to cut some people, places and things out of your life in order to address and deal with your own trauma. I made the decision to work on the split ends within, I have prayed, Journaled and even cried, but that wasn't enough.

    I needed Therapy often times we as Christians don't want to address the split ends within. We think it's ok to fake until we make it, however faking it until we make it is very damaging not just to ourselves but also to those who are inspired by our lives. We cannot expect issues to just dissipate because we're in church dancing and praising our God, all of that is Good because God requires us to praise and worship him, however

I am sure that he also wants us whole. Sometimes we think because we're Christians the issues will miraculously go away, because we dance, read, preach, sing and or pastor nope not at all. We need to heal. During that time of my life I needed to heal from the split ends within and go through the process of healing. That was the best decision that I could have ever made for myself.

And I am glad that The Lord was impressing upon me greatly to find a therapist, he knew what I needed more than I was aware off, why because he knows our beginning from our end and he knew what he had prepared for me to walk in and I would not be able to be effective helping others while I was steal dealing with the split ends within.

"My Therapist was God sent". Yes, I, a Christian of over 19 years during that time, needed Therapy. As I look back over my life and see how I am able to help others recognize that they also have split ends within and assist them through their healing and restoration journey it makes my journey all worth it.

I am not sharing with them something that I read in a book but something that I also experienced, because I could not have effectively testified without passing the test. There is no test without a testimony, now that I have cut my split ends from my crown and addressed and healed from the split ends within I can unashamedly unapologetically s.

The Prodigal

Prodigal is one who leaves home for a period of time and spends what they have recklessly as well as living their life aimlessly or in some cases living their lives without restrictions, there are many ways one can put a spin on the Prodigal, there are some that have left their homes in order to live freely without judgment from friends, colleagues or loved ones.

While children are growing they're personalities are also developing and shaping them to be uniquely them, this will also happen when children are exposed to various environments, however, there are also some rare situations that a child is just simply developing without influence, this can be a fortunate or unfortunate situation, however it is during those times when parents and guardians are unable to directly identify with particular behaviors that are being displayed, by the child and this leaves room for the child to be mislabeled.

As my children were growing up with their three different personalities and me myself being a teenage parent, I was extra protective of my children simply because I wanted to protect them. Seems to be innocent right? Well, I hate to be the barre of bad news, there are healthy ways to protect your child without leaving them traumatized. I learned the hard way when it came to me rearing my children and allowing them to be authentically them without any embarrassment, one of my children made the decision to explore the world. Literally! He disappeared without notice or a trace. I began to hear horrible stories about how he was living, and my heart would just ache. I was in disbelief that he was going through all of this. (did I raise him correctly?) And also, quite embarrassed because not my son. He totally disconnected from the family and was living as if he didn't have family or support. After a while he relocated from our home state and went on to the BIG APPLE, what was happening with him all along was that he was developing into himself, and he was no longer my little boy, but a young Man that was exploring life on his own terms and developing into who God created him to be by building his OWN testimony. (OUCHE)!

I received word that he was living in the state of his choice living recklessly, he would. call from time to time but not wanting to return back home. And when he did phone us, he was not sounding like himself, and I would just cringe and cry within, I didn't let him know that I was hurt, but I would also let him know how much I love him and miss him. With all of this going on I started doing

I can remember saying to God some years ago that I love him (GOD) more than I love the Children that he blessed me with. God requires us to love him more than anything and anyone. I don't know why I made that confession, because it has never come to mind before, but I did, and I confessed it out of my mouth. What I didn't realize was that I would be tested by my confession not many months later. And I was, my son disappeared and I had absolutely no idea where he was or what he was doing. I was frightened, during this time the Lord called me into the ministry. Serving his people and believing that he was taking care of my business as I was taking care of his, my confession still didn't't change. I love the Lord more than anything, my life is not my own, but to the Father I belong to. I trust him with the prodigal although I didn't see him with my natural eyes, I knew that God loves me and my son. My faith was elevated during that season of my life because I had nothing but my faith to sustain me. As time went on we began to put out flyers throughout social media praying that we would get a response from someone. Nothing, however, one day he sent his father a message and my heart was happy. We did speak with him, but he still refused to return to our home state.

I pleaded with him to return back because I was worried sick due to him not having a home to live in. One day I received a call from someone here in my state informing me that he was in NY with a stolen vehicle and the police in NY traced the owner of the vehicle back to our home state and he was sleeping in the car. I was so disappointed after that incident. I received a call from him informing me that he was incarcerated in NY. he was later released from prison and left NY driving down 95 South towards Florida and putting the police on a high-speed chase in and the vehicle crashed on the side of the highway, and then taking into custody and detained for twelve months, I booked a flight to Georgia and got him back to our home state and then he left again. Reminding myself this is a grown adult man.

Although he calls me and his grandmother from time to time, it's not the same, I often wonder how you can leave your family behind to live on the streets in another state with no family or friends. It is only by the grace of God that I am still holding on to the promises of God. I pray for him daily asking the Lord to protect and shield him from harm and danger and to ensure that he's eating and living in a safe environment. There are times when God will not respond to you in the way that you would like for him to return but knowing that he hears me carries from day to day. And with all that is taking place in my life with the Prodigal, my confession is still yes. Trusting the lord is not just something said to sound deep or righteous, but you must earnestly trust him even when you can't trace him and life makes absolutely no sense as to why you should trust. When you've done all, you can just stand, I am sure that there are many parents that are faced with waiting for their prodigal son or daughter to return home. Many have children that are incarceration, some struggling with substance abuse issues, abandonment issues, trauma, mental health issues or just simply out in the streets trying to find their own identity. One thing that I have learned is that the Lord is not slack concerning his promises. Allow your Children to be who God has created them to be with your guidance as a parent, don't place your identity on them or who you want them to be. The prodigal children are returning home.

ZERO

Where is she going with this one? I am glad you all asked, as we're all aware that the zero has no numerical value at all, it is the equivalent of naught, and the absence of a measurable quantity. The only way that zero will be able to have value is if there was something added to it. We often suffer at ZERO, because we have not yet come to the realization of who we really are, without being associated with a title, similar to these listed, Mother, Father, Son, Daughter, Pastor, Medical Doctor, Attorney, Police officer, the list can go on, we must know what our value is a person without being associated with a title. Knowing who you are is a liberating state to be in.

You will understand that you're deserving of peace of mind, love, comfort, longevity, wealth and healthy relationships. Decide to have zero tolerance for low hanging fruit, God's desire for our lives to live and abundant life and abundance in every area. I remember the day I realized that ZERO was no longer my portion in life, I began to add value to various areas of my life, my time, my peace. True identity will allow you to value who you are as a person, the person that God created you to be before any disruption came upon you, God said in Genesis 1: 26 let us make man in our own image after our likeness; and let them have dominion over the cattle, and over all the earth and over every creeping thing that creepeth upon the earth. So God did just that and value was added where there was no value, we were merely the dust of the earth until God decided to create us with his infamous wisdom. There is so much more to you.

We often get very perplexed when storms arrive in our lives and at times believe that the lord has abandoned us during the storm, however that is far from the truth. He trusts us in the storm already knowing the outcome of victory for our lives. There are storms that come upon us to blow the contamination and debris away from us, to help aid us into our true identity, however if we fail to manage the storm and get everything that was intended for us to receive the storm to manage us and we leave the storm incomplete and back at ground zero.

For the most part none of us like to suffer or be hit with the unknown, but keeping our trust in the Father and trusting the process that he's allowing us to go through will help us identify who we are. I realized that a balloon will remain in its manufactured state if it doesn't receive inflation from human breath or helium from the helium tank, but the moment that its inflated the balloon takes on the intended form with expansion, after that takes place, the balloon is now no longer zero meaning without substance, but now value has been added.

Tests and trials can sometimes leave you feeling invaluable when you go through them without understanding who you are as an individual or not getting the lesson out of the storm, the lord allows the storms and trials to come to us not because he desires for us to suffer during these storms, but so that we may learn who and what he is to us as his children remember one particular morning when as I was waking up from my sleep, there was a small Steele voice that said to "me meet me at the brook" I was a bit perplexed because I remember reading a passage from the bible in 1 King 17:4-6 were the Lord commanded Prophet Elijah to meet him near the brook. But to his surprise at the brook there was zero food stored up from him to eat, no refrigerator, deep freezer or any animals walking through that he could possibly kill for food.

It was zero provision from his own ability, but the Lord promised him that he will provide himdaily flesh (meat) and he could drink from the brook (lake) remembering that where the Father leads he will provide. I was excited that the lord would speak that to me, however when I accepted the invitation, I had no idea what that would be. Needless to say, I began to understand what ZERO meant.

When he went to the brook his ability to provide for himself was zero, he was sleeping outside and waiting for ravens to bring him breakfast and dinner and drinking his water from a brook. Waiting for the lord to command the raven to bring him flesh to eat. This is the exact place that the Lord needs for us to be where we totally rely on the Father to supply all of our needs according to Philippians 4:19 and my God shall supply all your needs according to his riches in Glory by Christ Jesus.

The place that the Father desires for us all to get is that we're out of our own options at ZERO and we can no longer make things happen, and we will submit to him as our Lord and not just our God. and depend on him to provide all that we need Genesis 22:14 And Abrahm called the name of that place Jehovah-Jireh: as it is said to this day, in the mount of the LORD it shall be seen.

Perfectionism My Story My Storm

Overcoming Perfectionism

1. Identifying who you are
2. Overcoming fear
3. Confronting Traumas
4. Unpacking preconceptions of self
5. Removing the masking
6. How did I get here?
7. Was this an inherited trait?

Some common insensitive mistakes:

(Telling others just get over it!'

(It's not that serious!

(I know what you're going through!

Breaking free from self-pity during the year of 2023 I was divinely transformed from the spirit of perfectionism, 2023 a significant year some said it was the year of completion and wholeness, well I will take that, after what transpired in my life during 2023. The nightmare and the burden of the need to be perfect in every area of my life faded away, whew! And I can now begin my new journey towards freedom, I was feeling like I was set free from the Pharo, because the burden and oppression that I was under for so many years was taxing on my mental as quiet as kept. Your girl was going through. I can finally exhale and inhale without restrictions. I was able to birth "Maria Speaks" were I release daily pearls of wisdom to the world; so many people's lives are being changed and transformed from my transparency, I was healed directly I the eyes of the people. I have gained the courage that I knew was locked down on the inside of me. I am perfectly flawed!

Psalms 139:14 For you created my inmost being you knit me together in my mother's womb, I will praise you because I am fearfully and wonderfully made: your works are wonderful I know that fully well.

About the Author

Maria Ushery is a Master Life Coach, Mentor, Speaker who empowers and encourages individuals that she comes in contact with on a daily basis she doesn't mind pushing and encouraging others in the marketplace, Church, as well as within the community, she's committed to leadership development, training and equipping those she's called to with her extensive coaching and mentorship background it is evident that she has the ability to push others closer towards their desired goals. She is also a Senior Pastor, Board Certified Christian Counselor, and Mother of three dynamic Children the founder of her annual empowerment conference for both men and women called the Process Conference and she also has a non-profit organization that was birthed in 2013 "Wailing Women" women of hope outreach, Inc. and the proud owner of Maria Ushery Coaching and Consulting Enterprises, LLC. and an Author. She is an over comer of perfectionism and colorism. Her favorite saying is "Change your mind, you change your life".

Made in the USA
Middletown, DE
13 March 2024